The Ordering of Stars

The Ordering of Stars

Poems

Kersten Christianson

Sheila-Na-Gig Editions

ISBN: 978-1-962405-52-2
Library of Congress Control Number: 2025951525

Sheila-Na-Gig Editions
Russell, KY
Hayley Mitchell Haugen, Editor
www.sheilanagigblog.com

Advance Praise

"Scavenged from the leafy / underbrush of thought," Kersten Christianson's rich word-hoard still leaves plenty of room for the inarticulate—raven tracks, moth wings, a screaming kettle—in this open-hearted and convivial collection. If, like me, you can't afford to visit Alaska, reading *The Ordering of Stars* might be the next best thing.

—Dave Bonta, author of *Ice Mountain: An Elegy*

Each poem in *The Ordering of Stars* whispers "Come-hither," invites the reader to a world in which the days move slower, in which life can be fully experienced in its most magical forms. In that sense, it is a spell book. The reader is transformed with each gentle moment, and the natural world will continue to sparkle even after the last poem is read.

—Lisa Stice, author of *From Reluctant Earth*

Acknowledgments

Alchemy & Miracles: "Chew on This," "Raspberry Nursery"

Capsule Stories: "Effloresce"

Cirque Journal: "Another Lunar New Year," "Revived by Fang & Claw"

Constellate; San Pedro River Review: "Resolve"

Foliate Oak: "Broken"

Mason Street: "Troubadour"

October Hill Magazine: "Of Paper Moons, Glimmered Words"

Red Alder Review: "Aurelia aurita"

Rituals: "Bring Corners Together to Fold the Kite Shape," "When the Chaotic Knave of Cleverness Calls"

San Pedro River Review: "Concentric"

Sea Wolf Journal: "Revived by Fang & Claw"

Sheila-Na-Gig online: "Another Lunar New Year," "Cosmic Harvesting," "Free Rent; No Lease Bingo," "I Never Knew," "Slice the Fruit Thin," "This Is Not a Love Poem," "Topography"

Sparks of Calliope: "Outer Coast Aubade"

Speculative Poetry: "Migration"

The Bluebird Word: "If Not Glitter, If Not Gold"

The Strategic Poet (Terrapin Books)*:* "Songbird, I Offer You Refuge"

The Wild Word: "Come-hither to the Hearth," "From the Outer Coast"

Tidal Echoes: "Before Snow Flies," "Heart as a Burning State," "Revived by Fang & Claw," "Tent's Collective Memory," "Trim"

Tiny Seed Literary Journal: "Flame's Return"

Tokyo Poetry Journal: "13 Considerations of a Blue Mussel Shell," "Like a Sniff of Pepper"

Trailer Park Quarterly: "At Night, Revisiting Our Dead Husbands"

Wingless Dreamer: "Bluebird, I Cannot Sing," "Tsuga of the Pine Family"

Young Ravens Literary Review: "Ode to the Coffee Grinder, My One True Love," "The Order of Birds"

In Gratitude

Over the moon with gratitude for the time, space, and creative nourishment gifted by Storyknife Writers Retreat in Homer, Alaska, and the Jenni House Artist Residency in Whitehorse, Yukon. Heartfelt thanks to directors, poet Erin Coughlin Hollowell and artist Janet Patterson, whose vision and hard work carve out such vital, wildy generative spaces for writers.

Thank you to artist and friend Susan Slocum Dyer, who painted *Thread and Stitch the Stars*—a constellation of color born mid-migration from Fairbanks, Alaska to Portland, Oregon. Gratitude also to poets Dave Bonta, MK Creel, Vivian Faith Prescott, and Lisa Stice for their generous words that lift this collection. To Sheila-Na-Gig editor, Hayley Mitchell Haugen—all the gold stars! Thank for you for sharing this collection with the poetry-reading world. I am so humbled.

Endless appreciation for the starshine inspiration of writers affiliated with Blue Canoe, *Alaska Women Speak*, the University of Alaska Low-Residency MFA program, and to my friends and family who are ever supportive of my writing endeavors.

Write on!

To all my favorite shenanigan shakers, kindlers of tomfoolery,
nothing but heart.

To Karen Cox and Gloria Luchinetti.

And to TH.

The sky a net, its mesh clogged with glowing stars.

Annie Proulx, *The Shipping News*

We are stardust
We are golden
And we've got to get ourselves
Back to the garden

Joni Mitchell, "Woodstock"

I'm restless. Things are calling me away.
My hair is being pulled by the stars again.

Anaïs Nin

Contents

III

IV

And So, It Begins

I gather the cobwebs spun
by long shadow storytellers.

Standing beneath a framed canopy
of dusk-darkened skies, I am ever

a falling fool at a fire-warmed hearth,
cherishing pinholes of dim daylight

through eroding leaves lingering
on baring branch. Leaf litter at my feet,

I step-shuffle a cryptic path through
bits of flame, crimson star shadow,

seasonal wandering under wind-
hollowed skies. If an hour can disappear

from the arms of a clock in November,
then I say bundle the silken threads of October,

pack gently among blue mussel shells,
cedar boughs, in a box marked autumn.

I.

Tent's Collective Memory

Outstretched birch boughs
branch for sky, arms gather
folds to locate two corners
of now. Snap of wrist,
of polyester, Big Agnes

takes flight. Wingless, swaying
an easy pitch, she has learned
an effortless bend, to lean
with the wind. Seam-taped,
like the uneven stitches,

the E6000 adhering heart,
this tent shelters from midges,
overnight gale, chill. Consider
bygone mornings waking
to a burled arm, curved leg,

slung over a body, two bodies
sleeping bag-baked, breath-mingled
warm. Two bodies cocooned,
silk-wormed light filtering limb
and fly. Our two bodies. One hand

meanders the mesh pocket holds
of another in love, jest, comfort.
Piled gear, Gorp, dried leaves
whisper hush the canvased walls,
the vestibule of now and then.

Heart as a burning state

i hail from the crimson Heart
tissue-papered organ: one-part sinew,
other sponge. tied by a stout butcher's
knot, one end knotted, the other
anchored, Heart scatters memories

in sepia: snapping campfire, twinkled
eye, morning lantern's light filtered
through mesh of branch, screen
of tent, trailed, feathered cirrus.
Heart is mapped by huckleberries

stippling the verdant branch, raspberries
dotting my palm like google map
markers; red, tear-dropped,
they travel measured, like a beat,
from tongue to belly. those from Heart

dwell in tiny homes with open-shuttered
windows, unlocked doors lead to light
and airy chambers. on a windowsill
perches a steller's jay, blue jar cobalt,
indigo plumed cry, its morning squawk

bellows to friends, would-be lovers.
for peanuts, it will sing a song;
for gooseberries, flight. soon, i'll pull
tent stakes, dry and flag-fold shelter,
shed this Heart—cultivate another.

Topography

Sometimes, you find yourself in the middle of nowhere. And
sometimes, in the middle of nowhere, you find yourself.

Where the Kitwanga
clutches the hand
of the Skeena,
begins the curved cut
north.

14 hours of conversation
with needled compass heart
and fly-by ditch daisies
in full bloom, I ask
their radiant faces,

Could he love
me? Could he
love me?

Make no mistake,
the nod-bob of their heads
as I fly by circle and star,
by return and guide.

Just shy of Good Hope
Lake sits the ghost town
Cassiar. Now abandoned,
it once carried the collective
hum of 50,000 worker bees:
Hockey rink, movie theater,
asbestos pit.

In Tā Ch'ilā Provincial Park,
turbid smoke from a nearby burn
meanders. Here, I navigate
the eskers and drumlins
of my own kindled hope.

Impermanence Is the Nature of All Things

The afternoon shines like a new penny; the road to Skagway, an eye-catching heads-up. Your daughter mailed you a package from home and when you arrive to the front of the line at the always-hopping post office, the post mistress says for everyone to hear, *Christ, still with the General Delivery? Get a post office box already!* She remembers you from six years prior, writing poetry in a cabin at the end of many roads. You remember drinking gin with her on the distillery's porch in Haines. When you gather your goods from home (disco twinkle lights, med refill, tiny shells, bits of beach glass), you tell her, *See you in another six years, friend!* From there, a stop at Jeff's bookstore to pick up new poetry from X̱'unei Lance Twitchell and Linda Buckley. At the pink gas station where you once heard a cruise ship bellowing "It's a Wonderful World," bouncing off mountains, the guy filling your tank with unleaded loves your turquoise and goldenrod earrings. So does Sarah, waiting in line with you for your pad Thai orders from the Starfire food truck. Fat Buddha sits between two blooms stretching their vitamin orange, their violet jam, for daylight through the cracks of the logging cable spool table, Fat Buddha with gleaming copper coins as tiny offerings at his toes. Back home, the summer's losses are immeasurable; your community's collective pain travels the channels of the Inside Passage clear up to the boreal and beyond. Fat Buddha would probably remind you there's never really an end, but a continuum, but maybe that's not good enough. Sometimes that woo-woo, that pluck, that mad energy is your only move, the reach and ponder of a found penny, heads or tails, lifted from the shrapnel-littered path.

Tutshi Lake picnic:
Noodles, wind, playing catch up
with my one-time husband.

In Their Falling

Stars need neither map
nor walking trail.
In their wandering,
they locate their point

of no return. Like deep
sea divers they tuck
in their chins, freefall
into depths both dark,

and unknown. What do
they find there? Pisces,
Capricornus, Cetus?
Or do they simply

drift on their backs,
bathe in the starlight
of their sky-roving
celestials?

Beach Twinkle

After Ada Limón's "Field Bling"

Tide when it's minus
and the beach seems still,
save the wash of lipper.
I walk the rimmed ebb
of rocky coast and consider
all the starfish.
I double-take, spotlight each
as if on a stage adorned
in lavender, sage, and coral tutus
and I pretend
they are sky ballerinas.
I call them
beach twinkle.
I call them
deep sea headliners.
I've not thought much lately
about following my departed
into his afterworld
of glitter and hue,
but I'm inspired again
to shed another skin,
armored bubble wrap,
to shimmy again with abandon
cast my coruscation to the wind,
to the nearest astral plane.

From the Outer Coast

A scallop plucked
from the low tide pool
held between two
fingers in wan
moonlight.

She explains
it has 200 eyes
primitive, rough,
silver beads stitched
in slick, orange mantle,
glowing in the headlamp's
reveal.

I ponder the puddled
memory of bivalved
wonder. Does she cling
to the rudimentary,
the tidal zone's ebb
and flow of picnic
and frost?

Do her eyes discern
a pattern? Here, love clings
to eel grass, propelled
by the tiny arms of sea
star larvae adrift
for 45 days.

In argent moonlight,
cupped in a curved palm,
a scallop returns to rocky
shoreline.

Broken

At Raven's Beach,
the dump of yesteryear,
you pick glass sliver shards,

pottered chunks adorned
with flecks of paint, a flower here,
a map there, a tiny ship way-

faring across the porcelain
sea of an artist's eye. A two-
legged elephant washed in patina,

rusty somethings covered in barnacles.
It's no wonder you name this margin
of coastline for the *corvidae*

whose own black bead eye
is drawn to the shiny cache
of a sunlit hoard. It's no

wonder your joy is rooted
in making what is broken
new, again.

The Windfall of Another Season

The mosquito coil of a warmer cycle
has burned down to its ashen core;
the long honey-light of day countered
by the sashay of darkening shadows.
In between the toppling of rain pelting
roof and pinpricked starlight, I sleep
in fits and stitches. With a bluster-snap
of wings, cranes, geese, and swans
companion south in V-formation; V
like *vault, vamoose,* and *vivre.* I fancy
their lengthy flight travels, the unraveled,
unspoken corkscrew of an apple skin's
peel, perhaps Honeycrisp, Granny Smith,
or Jonagold. Having eaten the dusty plum
beneath snap-saffron leaf, nothing
goes to waste.

Procession

The day is spent
in tumbling alder leaf
drop, removing the carnival
of birdfeeders from rollicking
maple trees. After a wash, a scrub,
they migrate to the garage
for a winter's rest. One returns
to its tree to offer seed (millet,
sunflower) to traveling songbirds,
winged minstrels pointed south.

Come-hither to the Hearth

On a day of gale, downpour,
leaf-drop, I invite the poem home
for a drink. This was no spontaneous

decision, but a well-thought plan.
It may have involved a wink,
a flash of leg, before ushering him in

through the front door, porch eaves
dripping a wild rhythm, staccatoed
by autumn wind blast. I drape his sodden

jacket over the arm of a chair to dry.
Perched on the sofa's edge he watches
as I spark candles, the small *psst* of kindle

plays against the jangle of ice and gin
in glasses emblazoned with a universe
of tiny saturns, shooting stars, moons.

Words bead along his tongue, scatter like seed
against the worn-wood surface of a paper-
cluttered desk. Dusk wraps its nighttime

woolen scarf around us while poem
whispers in my ear, makes no promises,
leaves a few words behind.

Slice the Fruit Thin

The cusp of autumn lands,
a golden crisped crust
of warming pear galette

drowning in the last light
feathering the stark ridgeline,
bend of an angel's wing,

between daylight and dark.
Pockets of ginger, cinnamon,
dust the echo of a day.

The knife's serrated blade
cuts and partitions sweet pie
without the hungered, sharp

snap of wolves waiting
in the wings, waiting.

Ode to the Coffee Grinder, My One True Love

By neither rhyme nor rule,
I sing twittery exaltations,
to painted ravens in frames,
a flight of larks without path
in an empty kitchen.

From poem to word,
whole to granular, bean
erodes to grain by hand.
I could open a window,
welcome the wind at my door,

set granule to flight to travel
zephyr's crest from rainforest
to coffee's faraway land of origin,
somewhere like India, or Peru.
Or I could shimmy hip to Nina

Simone, to screaming kettle,
dip and spin spoon, cream rising
the sun in the umbra of a mug
glazed to the shade and texture
of Bishop's Beach, early morning

sun between squall, cracking night.
Aroma of honeysuckle, dark chocolate,
lavender, meet the salt of outer coast
flood tide; pungent and meandering
in its wild.

Revived by Fang & Claw

The North Klondike Highway runs 330 miles from Whitehorse to Dawson City. The road braids its way through the boreal to meet, greet, and at times, offer tender, temporary goodbye to the Yukon River, before reuniting again with an open-mouthed kiss upon your arrival. You can't travel this artery without a finger on the pulse of memory. You remember his lazy, left-handed, two-fingered steer, windows open, his lower lip packed with Copenhagen Snuff, his right hand on your thigh, your hair blowing in the wind like a Bob Dylan song. Eyes wild, kindled by cuss and spark, loonies and toonies clanking in the console, not jazz, but Tragically Hip cranked on the stereo: radio / cassette / CD / streamed. This time, you trip this road like a missile, brake hard to watch Braeburn elk, iPhone photo-shoot a grizzly bear clawing through packed dirt and root for sun-worshipping ground squirrels. Even a deer catches your eye, and you marvel at this unscreened wild; no filter. Not even the acreage of still-smoking wildfire can slow you down. You have a 3:30 appointment with Double Denim Tattoo; Bee is ready to ink Zhùr, a 57,000-year-old wolf pup on the arm of your writing hand. A 57,000-year-old-wolf pup who still has stories to tell: That her last meal was salmon, that she was crushed in her den, that she still travels north from a museum display to attend Tr'ondëk Hwëch'in First Nations gatherings, like Moosehide. That she was found by miners in a goldfield outside of Dawson City. That she first appeared in a poem of yours in 2016, a haibun quite like this. And later, your finger traces this new art resting on a bed of flaming fireweed in your skin, you close your eyes and imagine the unruly nature of her copper pelt, that baby-soft animal fur of her. And later, you check into the magenta-trimmed Bunkhouse, walk the muddy, pot-holed street to the Back Alley Pizza Window. There, the old owner says to you in a thick, Italian accent, *Where is your man and your daughter?* as if no time had passed, as if seven years had not passed.

To answer, I grasp
at straws, the story too sad
for such fine pizza.

Refraction

On Sitka for Sale,
Gerta Wicket posted
a brass chandelier,
triple-tiered, layered
with pinned pendalogues,

crystals as luminous as birthday
cake, all its candles ablaze,
each a past life story of this
or that, a crescent of campfires
dotting the sphered shoreline

of memory. And of course,
I mulled it over too long
because $300 for brass
and glass seemed giddy,
and anyway, another

party expressed interest.
But out of curiosity,
I wandered to the Base
for her moving sale
where she told me,

Take it outside for a spin.
And in the sun, it spun,
and I was smitten with
its creak, dervish whirl,
ting of cut glass on glass.

Troubadour

Steve Miller belts
the "pompitous of love,"
and who even knows
what the hell that means?
He once performed
this song in the arena
behind student housing
through smoke and haze,
under field light, star light.

Light of heart, I've shimmied
to it, shared mingled breath
with another in darkened bars,
shaken bootie, not stirred,
around tables laden with glasses,
anchored haphazardly to wet rings,
soggy napkins. Glasses vesseling
fathoms, channeling ambered
uncertainties, opaque
braggadocios.

I've kindled rooms
with combustible laughter,
held captivated by ephemeral
memory of murky corners, right-
angled, and sweet. Lit by cedar
flame, stoked by driftwood,
I have burned feet to beat,
tripped the light fantastic to blur
the illuminated border of past
and present. I've strived
to carry love across.

Resolve

Oh, to be the dark-
eyed junco, wild
in its flitter, flap
through hemlock

branch, snow-
covered trunk.
To be driven,
resourceful

in the search
for seed, warmth,
shelter from squall
and bluster.

Migration

After "The Trees," by Adrienne Rich

The trees are moving inside again from the woods,
the timber that was abundant this year
with pine siskins
salmonberries
dark, ashen soil collecting rain these many days
will release root and empty.

All night the trees trail
mud-slithered tracks
long roots across the pecan floor.
Evergreen branches knock at the door
tap against the window pane
bow their crowns crossing the threshold
like the holy at an altar
present, stepping
into reverence.

I wait inside, door and window open to the gale
bead lines of words
related to anything but the transition
of woodland into the house.
The night is hopeful, the snow moon a satsuma
in a lapis sky
the scent of cedar bark and bough
wraps me like a Pendleton blanket.
Songbirds twitter in my mind
peck syllable seeds until pacified.

The Geography of Sweet Fruit

Satsuma Mandarins orbit
the cobalt skies of our northern December,
leap the yawning valley from peak-summer

to here-winter. Aloof stars lantern
the way. Brighter than LED twinkles,
their honey-tiger skin hangs loose,

pock-marked topography of moon caverns,
petroglyphs mark a short season of growth
and transpacific travel.

Give me no rigid lines, Cartographer—
neither longitude nor latitude—instead,
whorled circles, rounded mandalas,

a sphered tangerine whispering
a labyrinth of wonder in the palm of my hand
through that last juicy bite. Twirled by stem,

sometimes a poem can do that; sometimes
a poem can navigate the parallel boundary
of faraway and hearth.

Tsuga of the Pine Family

Soft-needled hemlock,
sculpted by edged breeze, you are
both branched, bare-barked, your

evergreen voice notes
a wooden, wild chime chanting
against trunked neighbor.

Tonal clopping, wood
on wood on wood, whispering
needle, shuffling dried

pages of gale, tea-
tossed fluttering paper, winged
winter hummingbirds.

Twinkled spell of fête, nip, rime,
you are welcome in our home.

II.

The Weekly Fortune Reads

In between gale and gust, 3+ 1 oracle
spread face down, humming on my page-
littered desk. The final crimson leaves
flit by the window with wings unseen
through a steam-storm of mugged, tongue-

burning cinnamon tea. Past, present, future,
+1 card for desire, for kicks. Having lived
so gloriously, the past is neither subject
to editing nor revision. I am no longer
interested dabbling in its message.

Chiseled in pale stone, the words made
vibrant with the rub of Kluane lakeshore
dust; sponged, dried, fading as it does
daily; a little or a lot. The present
and future a blend of solo wandering

bear cub, dream-blooming tangerine
poppies; ever-changing, seemingly
impossible, often hopeful. I have done
my due diligence, shuffled the deck
three times and cut.

If Not Glitter, If Not Gold

This early Sunday morning
my coffee mug steams.
A miniature Mauna Loa,
it resides within an archipelago

of trunk-top clutter: Solstice gifts,
dog-eared chapbooks, sun-bright
Satsumas. In this indigo light,
I scour Etsy for glitter-crusted

New Year banners, lunar calendars,
their moons of the year stamped
in bright gold, not just on paper,
but parchment. I can't explain

this fiery December need for
glimmer & glam, sparkle & flash,
but I am ever the believer, searcher
for the harbinger of fortune & joy.

Cheers to Another New

All the quirks of the season—
darkness, glitter, storms without reason—

and we're right back at another beginning;
still, that feeling of closing one door

to open another, could be the closest experience
to magic happening, if only in the unpackaging

of a spanking new calendar, its pages crisp
and unturned, and in the square numbered

one, I put my daughter on flight 62 to veer south
again to her college town, drive out by Whale Park

to pick up my weekly veggie box (mandarins,
leafy lettuce, cherry tomatoes), pull over to celebrate

news that a poet friend shares of an upcoming collection
to be published, and the juncos and their tiny friends flock

to the feeders, to the birdseed I spill on the driveway,
and these are the hours and actions that warrant

welcoming the new: upswing of light, lighter step,
stepping into all that might shimmer and shine.

At Night, Revisiting Our Dead Husbands

After Ada Limón's "Midnight, Talking About Our Exes"

The sky is bright as if mid-afternoon.
Two foxes, one cross, one silver, play
freeze tag on the stairs and porch
of an empty school entry, romp
into the blankness of a full-mooned
whiteout, territorial hunters
on this gale-swept plain.

(Or what we name the way
we move forward.)

Let's be foxes tonight, or foxy,
venture from our dens of silent walls,
skirt roadside clearings, wild-eyed
and curious of all the other
beyond what we once had.
All of our chase and cajole
cannot hush the anguish of death
nor can time.
When all that remains is the hour,
let us be the poems of survival,
let us cavort in our wild
under the dimmed outline
of circumstantial stars.

Aurelia aurita

Again, sleepless night.
In a last-ditch leap, my mind
          conjures pirouettes,

moon jellies, drift-drawn
          in the azure splash of tide
embracing river's

mouth. Wait. Gathering
          bloom by swell, clenched translucent
bell, bombastic slip, slide

into blue night's rise.
          My wake silhouettes, sunsets
          under a blanket

of aching stars. Auspicious
          in their flickering, sleep comes.

13 Considerations of a Blue Mussel Shell

Victim of sea stars,
it serves a shallow spoon
for crab chowder.
A cup full of blue
to loan to misty skies
to remind us of the value
of clear, and bright.
A bowl for collecting
rippled sea glass,
the shiny bend, riffle
that catches our eye
and ear, like stars, moon,
the shuffle of playing
cards, and galaxy.
A shovel to bury
our happiness
in the yard, to dig
up later, when blue.

According to the Mystic, or, Fortuitous

Like mooncakes in winter,
and a clock without numbers,
fortune is sometimes questionable
in all its hats, jackets,
and fleece mittens.

Sometimes it knocks
at the door, a swift-knuckled
rap, an option wrapped
in all its finery, confidence,
and who wears it best.

Sometimes it visits
as if attending a reception
masked in cat eyes,
sequins, a few tucked-in
feathers dyed fuchsia.

And every now and then
it lands with a slam
like an epiphany, wisdom
undisguised, blatant
and nude.

Fortune serves mooncakes
at the lunar reception.
We wear our moonboots.

When Even the Astrologer Says You're Fucked

Connect-the-dots, you trace
the lines of constellations
with a dull-tipped pencil.

Squint! A sun bear,
a mariner's astrolabe,
a rainforest's bracken!

The night sky is a hand blown
water glass replete with ambient
kindness, and you question

the message, as you would,
the paper fortune wrapped
in a cookie, or the head side

of a penny found at your feet.
The struggle is real, reckoning
which star to pluck, to burnish

warm copper with steel
wool and some lemon juice.
But when that scrubbing

turns tempest, elbow grease
and gale, you shift gears
from wondering where the leap

of luck went wrong, and laugh
that sometimes shiny still glimmers,
kindled rose under all that patina.

Placebo Effect, or Fact?

When the local apothecary
advertised an herbal love potion
my girl and I butterfly-fluttered
our winter-rose wings
down to the local shop
in Sunday-shivering downpour
to procure bottled tincture

(Lemon Balm, Ginger);

wild elixir cradled
in the palm of a hand.
Admittedly, I'll pay fierce penny
for any kind of good fortune,
too often absent in this world:
any kind of Lady Luck that gifts
happiness, love, and freedom

(Damiana, Hawthorn).

Memento on my tongue,
my testimony stands:
an upcoming breakfast date
for me, a thousand dollar
check the next day for the girl?
My heart softens with wonder
and delight

(Meadowsweet, Clove).

sometimes the stars need
aligning with a crescent
wrench. Or a hammer.

Waylaid by Scrimmage and Sound

Hum of wing, of scream
braided flight call, in short, sharp
whistle. Churring rust,

flash of indigo,
morning waxes boreal,
of winterberries,

of clustered starfruit
lingering on my tongue. He
showed me his bird guide,

belted kingfisher
penned in Arabic by hand,
low-flying cursive.

Yes, to age-honeyed photos,
to desert sun-squinted eyes.

Another Lunar New Year

and I find myself in the bughouse,
again, my heart in my eyes, and buzzing
through the door at the Elks on a Friday night
for his chicken lo mein and eggrolls.
It's the Year of the Dragon,

and my monsters are nothing
but ardent. Bright-eyed and amorous
they are fiery-tongued, and word-slipped
as they tend to be in flatlined winter.
When his shift is over, and he's

ordered a pint, I pat the barstool
next to me, settle in close for stories,
and his good company. We're not public
like this, it's a first, but he's a dimber cove,
and I tease him that without my readers

he could be the actor Jeremy Allan White
of Calvin Klein ad fame, only his older, hotter
brother, rooftop cavorting in his skivvies,
his arms stretching for the blaze, reaching
for me in sizzling moments. He tells me

it's time I had my eyes checked. He's no
quick smiler, but his hand touches my arm, shoulder,
every time I think he will. And later, when I text him
thank you, his fiery reply, *'Night beautiful!*
keeps me smitten; keeps me warm.

I Never Knew

My winter-fall lover
reads books of wild birds
and Alaska, while I plumage
through Canada, take up Lorna

Crozier's assemblage of "Sex
Lives of Vegetables" and other
audible, poetic fêtes. Juniper
and orange drift from the stink

pot. These oils, the essential
reminder of spring-soon-to-come,
drift through time-standstill
of Saturday afternoon laze,

rare sun, and cherry martinis.
I know now why the poet
Cisneros lifts her lovers up
in poetry.

Outer Coast Aubade

From sea to sky
blue heron stretches,

pulls at the strings
of the harvest moon

tugs the night closed
like a shade.

Oh heron, stretch
and pluck wayward stars

Drop them in my clam
bucket, so they clang

like metal spoons,
so that I may take them home

and one by one bestow
my wishes in hushed

night tones. Spoon and
chowder and stars. Oh, heron,

promise me an open
window. Promise me the dawn.

III.

a honeyed note penned
at the tangled edge of hope.
Heron's blue feather

Bluebird, I Cannot Sing

Even the Mountain
Bluebirds detour
from their path.

Spring migrators,
they parallel the coast,
fly to the pull of the moon
and the beryl tide.

Blue, this morning, a throng
of 15 gathers on branched
snag at the Mendenhall.

Blue, their bodies, blue
as cosmos, stipple
the dried mosses
of winter.

Blue, they perch
on weather-worn wood.
Breeze ruffling feather,

they trill, mewl the broken
notes of a love song.
It is said the female
chooses her mate

for the nest he'll
provide; neither song,
nor look, nor the way
his wings take flight.

When the Chaotic Knave of Cleverness Calls

When the curtain cloud opens to reveal nothing but clear, night sky, your gal pal Gloria wanders over to share stories of love and crime, and a bottle of cabernet. It's her 70th spin around the sun. Between the two of you, there's enough silver-gray hair to loan some to sky, wispy tendrils to entangle stars, pluck them down to land among one foolish-heart project, or another. Her wild creativity has called again, her muse a frolicking imp of needle and thread. She has stitched postcard panels of tiny deer among embroidered trees under the poet-coddled moon. Could this be a haiku without words? You chat haiku, its identity of nature, breath, both present and presence; of Basho's long wander along a narrow wriggle of road, ambling north, pausing only when the urge to integrate community with writing became too strong to ignore. They say poetry is a bit like lightning; you're obligated to strike, to toss words down on thin page in the interim between flash of light and crash of thunder. And that's all good and fine, but you live on the outer coast and lightning is a rarity, seldom viewed. So maybe here, poetry is metered out more within the space between a whale's heartbeat and breathy exhale. You rehearse the potential line between imagined beat and release, the surrounding ocean filled with pages of all the poems that have been and those yet to become.

Later, adrift, dream
of long-stitched vowels, consonants
threaded, finger-traced.

Behold, the Swamp Lantern

We daily drive to Starrigavin
to eyeball the estuary
where the swans reside
in wintertide before
continuing their trek
north.

At the turnaround,
your daughter points
out the window, says,
Look! Skunk Cabbage!
laughs when you brake
hopeful-hard at her ruse.

This is the day we yearn
for such fresh color, kiss
of sun yellow to ground,
an uprising and rebellion
of green shoots announcing
their return.

Like a Sniff of Pepper

All our passwords
contain 0439, the combination
of his lucky number, and mine.

I can share this in an unpublished
poem, assured that it won't be thieved
by a migrating robin, or a thrush,

too busy unlocking the newly-
warmed earth for grub and worm.
When the poet asked, *Do you look*

east or west for word-ly inspiration?
I consider the glass star candleholder.
High on the shelf, its rounded face
seeks only the Hyperborean, lost
galaxy, while shimmer-pole dancing
to blanched tealight through the late-night

hour. My scarf packed away for the season,
buds detonate from the corkscrew willow,
pesky alder, prickled salmonberry;

soon, leaf-ing. I know little of explosives,
of spruce bursting pollen blooms,
of playing the hand I've been dealt,

but I know that love, like grief,
comes on like the tickle of a sneeze:
Quiet, unexpected, sudden.

Free Rent; No Lease Bingo

B	I	N
B is for Bystander and you are your own	I is for Introvert and you fly this like a flag in a March williwaw	N is for No for all the times you wished you'd said yes
Standing at the end of the bar, gin & tonic half-full/empty, wet ring pooling on varnished wood	So that other introverts feel safe to approach and visit in their comfort zone, the quieter, the better	Read your poetry to an audience in a bar, at a gathering, on a stage
Not even ice melting in glass catches the flash of disco ball prisms sparkling	Phone calling isn't your thing, you feel you jabber, or mute and overthink what should have been said	Rent is FREE When You Live Inside Your Head
Standing out of range of microscopic chatter, bright orb	And lean on voice mail to collect, sift, and deliver moments of minutiae	Travel with him to Iceland to circle the Ring Road, look for trolls
You can imagine the freeing shake of loose hip, flip of hair to Gloria Gaynor in the helix	And you've stopped shaking hands as way of introduction since the pandemic	Go to all the community events: the chowders, frybreads, grinds and ramshackles

G	O
Gravitate to the silence that offers peace	O is for Ongoing Distractions, the Netflix show that is a 2 and not a 10
To the wind that muffles noise and fills your ears with stories	The early to bed and late to rise; early to work and first to leave and quick to skip a meeting
To the low tide without other walkers, sun low on the horizon	Piles of books that drift below dreams under pillows, tangled in bedding
To the bookstore packed with all your not-yet-acquainted favorites	The 4 am Wordle in lieu of French-pressed coffee
To the friends who welcome your quiet arrivals and sudden departures	And your words forging a raven's tracks across the page

With an armful of possibility,

false spring knocks at the door:
Linger-longer daylight hours,
daffodil starts stretch for new vision,
the sun blazes a brighter torch
than the day before, and even
the day before that.
I walk this kindled path,

rutted by my long-abandoned
flowerbeds to dream again
of their wild possibility.
Frozen in memory,
they once brimmed
with bud, bloom and seed:

Blue poppy,
            clematis,
                        nasturtium.

A joyful grind, I once tended
this patch of color as if family—
matcha tea green, verdant—
now the scraggly vines catapult
their stone barriers, remind me
of what I've neglected;
of what can thrive again.

Flame's Return

In March I hanker
for the fireweed huddled
in packed, frozen ground.

Like a red robin,
my ear imagines stirrings,
a humming refrain

beckoning green growth.
Tapping taproot, forked and branched.
A first sip of tea,

I want to observe
its annual emergence,
tender shoots straining

for light-lengthening skies, for
another round of wild growth.

Cosmic Harvesting

Not quite lucky wishbone
nor water divining rod,
but there it sat like a stone,

a discarded moose leg in the road
at the corner of the Carcross
Community Center.

It made me think of Gloria's
moose hoof windchimes,
heavy keratin *clop-clopping*

in the wind as if still plodding
through knee-high grass, fireweed,
one foot trailing another, wood-throaty

like bamboo, strung with blue-eyed
beads, tinny silver bells. I read recently
that sometimes a tuft of green

hair can be found near a moose's
hoof. I wanted to turn around,
drive the grizzly-road back

to Carcross, to look more closely
for this anomaly, this flash
of cut tendon, bone, early leaf.

There Is Solace, There Is Flow

There are words you can only shout into the hum of a Sunday morning: *Venus, Defiance, Blip.* In flight, gulls advance, retreat, their wings forged silver by sun bounced off ocean blues, cloud pewters. One neighbor has retied their hammock to billow between two stout alder trees, it is flutter and eye-catch; the other floats his welcome to the morning from his deck-spot hot tub within view of L'úx, the long-dormant volcano. Here, at your small reign of desk, your gone-rogue hair waterfalls down your back. It will experience the taming of neither brush nor comb this day. There is the splendor of coffee steam and your dad's smoked salmon for breakfast; the bitter bite of brew and fire on your tongue. It's all a bit extrasensory, really, especially for such an early morning start, windows open to collect the song-crack of wind. Seedlings of words disappear from your mind, leap to paper, shuffle down, down, down the page, much like the drop and *plunk* of nasturtium seeds from paper packet to soil later this day to map a much later bloom, much like the rain that was supposed to fall this day and has not yet. There are houseplants to water, oracle cards to draw, dog-eared books to read. Wing tip to tide, the gulls circle Guide Island, follow the wake of the *Kestrel* north, and you close with a haiku.

> *Write while the sun shines*
> *bright, to the lemon-yellow*
> *mug, to the morning.*

Chew On This

Lured by the light—
bisque, lemonish,
pie crust warm—
I rise and stretch
under the sharp-edged

April sun as it glances
along the glass surface
of storm-dirty windows.
I could hold this glint
like a lover, brush

back its shadows
like an errant lock
of hair on its hooded
brow. Or, I could
walk the perimeter

of my yard, rake winter's
leavings, welcome—
as if kinfolk—
the first flush bloom
of salmonberry.

The Order of Birds

First line credit to the poet Joy Harjo

Birds are singing the sky into place. Dipper, robin, sparrow; my mornings begin before the wink of daylight, to *flit, chip, twitter, buzz,* a cacophony of songbird riot among bare-branched alders, cedar boughs, chaos ringing in my ears. Forgetting they fly, bird shadows chase across the mossy yard, weave in and under last season's raspberry canes on skinny legs, delicate feet. Some money in my pocket, some money in my pocket, I wear hammered silver raincloud earrings with indigo Russian trade beads, tiny rain chains downpour as it does here all too frequently. Have I bartered baubles for the shroud covering the morning set moon? Have I jinxed the chance of a warming April sun?

> *Soon, hummingbirds drink*
> *from salmonberry blossom;*
> *from columbine bloom.*

Raspberry Nursery

Before the red maple leafed,
while fiddleheads unfurled,
raspberry seedlings jumped
the border of their bed,
hummed and wriggled their way
through dense winter ground.
Sunlight, wan like egg drop
soup, guided their efforts;
mossy yard buffered
their seasonal stretch
through slushed rain.

In early May gust, they hitched
tiny, branched arms to sky,
and danced.

Under a plume of drizzle,
trowels in hand, my lover and I
leave knee prints in the soft ground,
unearthing each start and its root,
carefully avoiding mingled fireweed.
With muddied hands, we place
each in buckets to transplant
from my yard to his. He looks
forward to his young neighbor, Otto,
checking for berries, while I delight
in this other use of his lithe hands,
his careful placement of found snail
onto a safer patch of ground,
with a, *Hey, little guy…*

There are only so many days
of spring before they dissolve
into memory: Mud, hands, root,
start; hint of fruit in days to come.

First the Flower, Then the Fruit

The rules of salmonberry bloom
are unforgettably simple. First,
be willing to root. Search among

the spindle of thorned cane and stalk,
your bright bud hunger soothed only
by the branch brimming an emergency

of salmon, flamingo, taffy. This hue,
long-absent, arrives homeless,
seeking no shelter from the recurrent

eclipse of squall gunning hail pellets
against window glass, painted bunting.
Second, let your ache drive your gaze.

Cup fledgling starburst in your palm;
know what it is to hold a constellation,
a thicket of five-petaled stars, in your hand.

She Is Her Own Wild Creature

My rising is slow this blustery day. An hour behind, one hour ahead, it's my girl's birthday. I'm juggling three clamshells of lucid thought: that she is my greatest joy, that 19 would have been her dad's next favorite year of her, that I never went into labor; her birth, instead, a concoction of Greg Brown, *Law & Order*, Diet Coke, and upon earthside, her first breath, "Red Dirt Girl," by Emmy Lou Harris. Aside from vomiting on my compassionate nurse when she told me a story of a three-nippled woman trying to breastfeed, and raising my hospital bed too quickly after, the c-section was a breeze and I was walking this new girl baby in Totem Park days later as if, like a starfish, she were a fresh appendage I'd grown. Motherhood gives us all a touch of refugee status as we depart; the old life we occupied trails behind as if a wake, for the status newly offered. Those changes, wavelengths both subtle and profound, undulate like seagrass in current. My girl is adamant in her interests, forever the outlet of ocean, the many-eyed scallop, the tiniest of starfish nestled in the palm of her hand. If she were to choose an avatar, I'm hard-pressed to guess her choice: Narwhale, humpback, or barnacle?

> *Untrapped, unfettered,*
> *the cut and glide of a kayak*
> *through a blue-papered sea.*

Birds, Balloons & Birkenstocks

Because it's nearly bright break,
bouts of binging balm and Bingo,
I brake for buttery baked bread

and bewilderment; bumblebees
and bliss. Boundless in this brief,
buzzing bucket of buoyancy,

I bibble-babble, banter with books
and their bibliomaniacs, burst
among blue, bright-eyed blossoms

that backbone barriers of boulevards
and bystreets where errant balloons
brush up against bridge beams, birds

bounce boldly from branch to branch,
and I am ballsy, bodacious, burgeoning
on bountiful earth and best Birkenstocks.

The Leeward Side of the Mountain

Late summer density, a pending front
undulates, weaves through high valleys,
to hover among crags and peaks. I'm no
orographer, but when it rains, it floods,
enough buckets of tears to drop, slide,
shift mountains thought otherwise solid.
Weeks of *nagging, cajoling, reminders*
to pack this, clean that, don't forget...,
and she's gone on a southbound ferry.
Occasional photos land by text: eye-level
sunset clearing the ferry's rail, washing
the tent's interior in light; the cat, five-days
kenneled, pacing new space; used Fiestaware
in ROYGBIV stacked on a knick-knack table
in a secondhand store. I'm not certain why
I've chosen to stay on in this empty house
of echo and memory, to wash my one used dish
after each meal, pursue his encouragement
of Elks membership, tinker away at a new job.
I hold my fortunes close, used to Scotch tape
them in a journal I burned on Bishop's Beach
in Homer. Now these paper harbingers, fluke
of written-word kismet, fortune, and numbers,
are stored in the bowl-shallow saucers
of lenticular clouds, organized by wonder-luck,
repetition, and by the grammatically incorrect.
I hold my fortunes close, paper, or otherwise,
and wonder where I'll wander in a year.

IV.

Effloresce

Today I broke the spine
of Mary Oliver's *A Poetry Handbook*.
while contemplating sound and device.

My finger traces its even seam, words lay
down like train track—aligned, avoiding dips,
spikes driven gently into the heartwood

of their meaning. The book's crack,
crumble, an alliterative soundtrack to the dog
outside eating dandelion greens

before their orgasm of bloom and seed.
And if this annual coming of bud and scatter
carries any real resonance, I imagine it

to moan like the night buoy at sea:
rounded, breathy, prolonged— late
into the dark morning hour.

It is book. It is paper. It is leaf.
Verdant, temporary, I ask,
Who hungers for you?

Heart Like a Bullseye

—First line borrowed from the poet Morgan Parker

I am saving for you / a sharpened arrowhead / for luck and practicality
You may delight / in its flecked intention / cliff-cragged hope
The letter *A* trailheads / the words *Accuracy, Ace* / *Atlatl*
Organic in its blue feather throat / caribou tendon / birch sap
We ache / from spear's tangled pierce / from heart shatter
Our living, a litter of lynx / herd of caribou / flock of swallows
Captive time travelers / frozen by moon-span / fixed by ice patch
The deception lies / in its stillness / this is no meandering glacier
I carry this image of you / your palm cupping my cheek / your eyes
Flash summer lightning / Ross River emerald / spun fireweed silk
Discarded / cracked and weathered / this sling has no give.

And When We Talk About Bears

And there they traipse: sow,
her two cubs; their henna hides
ripple as their thick

bodies carve a wake
through verdant sedge of ocean-
side estuary. Bright

dahlias, russet bloom,
brown bears ebb and flow like tide
their short bloom sustained

by mixed greens and soon-berries;
to later feast on red-fleshed
salmon. For now, cubs standing

on short, rear legs. Mouths chock-full
of what sustains. Small faces upturned,
their short season warmed by evening sun.

Bring Corners Together to Fold the Kite Shape

We write about blue,
the folding of 1,000 paper cranes,
of thievery in the Garden of the Sun.

I'll confess, I no longer remember
the steps of intricate fold and crease
to morph thin Kami paper into bird,

but my memory's eye recalls
its open stretch of wings, launch,
sudden break, meteoric glide

through flickered light shadow, wing-
skimming the sky-open faces
of Himalayan blue poppies, forget-

me-nots, the unfurling mandalas
of Fiddlehead greens, to glide descent,
to settle on bench. I confide, I know not

what this paper-winged thief lifted
from the garden, be it bloom,
be it bounty (silken web, lucky penny,

hummingbird's nest). What remains
unanswered keeps us curious;
keeps us bold.

Songbird, I Offer You Refuge

For the poet John Haines (1924-2011)

Of cracked, weathered wood, aged by freeze and thaw, hewn
by hand, eye, of plain shape: box, arrow's point, full moon,
assembled with rusted, mismatched screws, crude shelter
for songbird of trill, *jid-it,* hover and flutter;

the poet once scrawled words across the parchment peel
of paper birch trees, cast lines of poems piecemeal
to the sky, carried by ruby-crowned kinglets
migrating north for another season, ringlets

gathered to construct nests of twigs, spider webs, moss,
lined by conifer needles, feathers, down, crisscrossed
with the poet's own craft of homesteading: Amble
the long road north, clear forest, cut trail, haggle

stout roof upon four walls, carve a door facing south;
an ear for sweet bird-verse, a page for word of mouth.

Of Paper Moons, Glimmered Words

Each night I stand under the cheese-white moon,
utter orisons to pin-pricked starlight
beneath the maple leaning in full swoon.
I want to gather blossomed words to write
bud and bloom, bird-seeded words taking flight,
landing, a flurry of moth wings, on page
smooth as cherry tomato skin, warmed, aged
in lazy July afternoons, high sun
chasing moon beyond darkness, circled stage
of lush green earth, cursive script, madly spun.

Pondering Blue at the Mile 1016 Pub
in the Junction

"Pompeii Excavation Unveils Rare 'Blue Room' Believed to
Be an Ancient Shrine."—Leah Sarnoff, ABC News

I have a fixation
on old things: wolf
pups, baby wooly
mammoths, and rooms
in blue scrawled
with seasons.

Just last weekend,
I placed a string
of wooden trade beads
Bruce found on the tundra
near Shaktoolik
in the hands of friends

who also marveled
at the things we can't
put a date on. Today,
I considered blue
as I discarded the thick-
knit sweater

of coastal precipitation
for the tranquility
of robin's egg sky
not so unlike the blue
pine floor at home,
both distressed, bright.

I could tattoo upon both
floor and sky words
of Fortymile gold dust,

Yukon cavorting, and love
along a muddy river
both roiling, swift.

Wolf pups and mammoths;
earth and sky; ink of Himalayan
poppies, blueberries flow
from the poet's needle.
Blue is a holy place,
a gathering of words.

Like *Babette's Feast*

After harvesting catch,
mugs of bitter coffee,
shower, afternoon nap,
we transfer rainwater-
soaked cedar plank
from bucket to grill.
June sun filters steam

and when hot to touch
king salmon fillet slides
skin to wood. Brushed
in walnut oil, we close
the lid, create a sauna
bake while preparing

the rest of the meal:
steamed asparagus,
thick-sliced
garlic bread,
sweet and sour
calico beans.
By the time we set

the mineral blue dishes
around the island, fold
napkins, fill water
glasses, fat drips
from fish now bronzed
in hues of tea leaf,
henna, the summer
stop of time.

Could Have Been

Those slate streets of Vancouver
my feet pounding pavement, wrapping
around the corners of one gritty-hard block

into the next. Marigolds in their saffron
dresses lean over their metal fences of breeze-
creaking baskets, bright swinging constellations,

their gaze a boom against blue sky. Or maybe
wave-kissed Francois Lake, thunderstorm
rolling across distant peaks, knee-deep

in current, my legs a mooring, safe harbor
in the larger lagoon of here, or there. I carry
a spool of loose threads wherever I go;

bits and pieces of memory like photos washed-
out by time. An ear open for new stories,
nothing is left threadbare.

Trim

Lyrics borrowed from ABBA's song "Fernando."

Fernando the hairdresser
takes walk-ins.
After 8 weeks
on the road

I am all too happy
to have him weed-
whack my bangs,
clear cut along the ridge

of my worry lines
that lighten
in the airy shade
of birch trees.

In the airy shade
of birch trees,
I hum the old ABBA
song, "Fernando."

Some of the lyrics
are lost upon me,
these holes filled
with crinkling leaves,

footsteps on a gravel
path, the ebb and swirl
of the Yukon River.
Fernando the hairdresser

doesn't charge for bangs.
I shake his hand, instead,
leave his shop light

in step, my wings clipped,
I could fly again:
There was something in the air
that night, the stars were bright,
Fernando.

grace for the *ursus arctos horribilis*

may the forest
sheltering any number
of human malfeasance

shuffle gentle breeze
against your upturned face
may you stretch your limbs

in the wind, invite warm sun
to caress your shoulders as you
change direction to exit a door

that was never yours to open   may
you recognize with open heart, clear
conscience, this lush dwelling

of birch, black spruce, of ursine
wandering their hallways, teaching
their young the sweetness of their world:

dandelion greens, berries and roots,
salmon's crimson flesh   may
you offer them wide berth

Fall Down Eight Times; Get Up Nine

Tuesday, and it's Wing Night at the Kopper King Neighbors Pub on the outskirts of town. $9.15 a pound, eat-in only. I give this menu a sidelong look, once believed the place to have been a magnificent steakhouse we never stopped at for one reason or another, only to learn its depth is quite shallow: Wings, domestic bottle beer, low-light dingy. I spent the whole of Monday in the lantern glow of the Old Snow Carver and his longtime Yukon stories. He once sold me a Raven Lady in full crouch, shoulders stout enough to carry the world, to carry my man from this lifetime to another. Like a farfetched Greek origin tale, Survival birthed from Absence and this Raven Lady took up residence on my desk as only a muse can. As we sipped cranberry and lavender radlers from Yukon Brewing, he spouted stories of ice carving competitions in Quebec and Japan, of reading the weather for CBC and our common joy for words like *graupel*, how his first wife left him with two babies to raise, how it's possible to recover from most kinds of slip. We exhaled over shared insight of creative process while his hands shaped and molded a new Raven Lady for me. When he asked me what characteristics she should have, I first tried to shrug off the inquiry as I'm introvert-inclined, but forged into what I secretly hoped would emerge: Big-breasted, on her knees provocative, head tilted, fiery hope and flirt and humor in her eyes. There is glazing and firing yet to do. Will she carry shades of shadow plum or Poseidon teal? How the arms take to flame will determine her outcome. I may not remember that Tuesday is Wing Night at the Kopper King, and I don't really care about that, but I'll never forget how Donald Watt's hands forged flight from a block of clay in a Monday cabin.

> *Raven Lady guards my desk*
> *like a shiny thing;*
> *a lucky penny bauble.*

Before Snow Flies

Consider the road-tripped
morning, sleeved Americano,
parfait with all things homegrown:
granola, yogurt, berries; or your love,
and the daughter you grew from seed,
all sprout and tangled wildflower.

These you savor in the shadow of thought,
of an unknown mountain, and another, another.
Kaslo, Kokanee, Nakusp—you trip kilometers
between Canada Day festivals, hot springs,
music in the park to campgrounds; tents
and campers festooned with twinkle lights,
bonfires, bottle cap, can tab chatter.

How are you to remember? How are you
to pool the collective memory of two,
of place and detail? How do you share
the stories that took wing-spread flight
from his mouth, Red-tailed Hawk
to current? Given years and loss,
what have you already forgotten?

It is not the dry sweep of wooden boardwalk,
thin paper of Japanese lanterns, of knotty wood
formed broomstick, of coffee and book,
of bobbing hot pools in direct sun. Nor
is it your bodies, curved parentheses warming
the baby in between, curved in sleep, bagged
in tent at the cooling edge of this lake,
or another, and another.

These Love Songs

After Robert Hass' "That Music," from Time and Materials

The river's gurgle and chomp of late July
Outside our sun-high tent without fly, its bubble
and bite of mud-kissed bank, a tangle of Alaska
paper birch, balsam poplar, trembling aspen,

Current and wind—, do they whisper
In morning's broad light, his voice in her ear,
Whisper—, do wind and current meet in root or leaf?
If you were the translator, your task is to find the words.

This Is Not a Love Poem

It rains in Whitehorse
and children still frequent-flood
the playground, their screams,

laughter, a raucous
murder of ravens mid-hop,
feigned flight. And because

it rains in Whitehorse,
I ache to scrawl love poems
for my not-in-love,

whisper in his ear
the beauty of dried morels,
spicy dill pickles,

northern gifts soon delivered
to where I'll find him waiting.

Curiosity Piqued

When you come across a single moose leg at the intersection and wonder the walking whereabouts of the remaining three; this could be a constellation, or a parable. That you listen to old country and the weekly Indigenous music chart toppers. That you spend an evening watching robin chase squirrel from nest, down trunk, through the July underbrush of absinthe and fresh celery green. When you take time to smell the wild Yukon roses in their throat-opening bloom, a Dairy Queen Blizzard in your hand. That lilacs and fireweed blooming simultaneously can alter the taste of honey. That a wasp is not a bee, the evidence of that, the stinger in your thumb. Even this, a blessing.

Concentric

Well-trodden walking path;
5,000 steps round and round
the crusted path of a Pizzelle.

Warm-walled yurt floored
with a medallion tapestry,
kaleidoscopic orb of colors.

Small town roundabout
slows to a caution, brings
a spring carnival Ferris wheel-

squealing, rotating happy circles.
Escape hatch into a poem
lurking just below the surface.

Old growth yellow cedar
stump, its zodiac of tree
rings come to an and.

Red huckleberry stacked
on a slice of kiwi, zucchini,
lemon, and orange,

balance-beamed
on a half-cantaloupe.
Lid to the soup pot,

bowl of raspberries,
rotary dial, roaming
eye of the halibut,

pupil shuttered
by iris. The end.
Period.

About the Cover Artist

Susan Slocum Dyer is what is called a "transplant Alaskan." Her home city is Boston. She is a lower elementary, public-school teacher who has taught in high-needs villages across Alaska, including 350 miles above the Arctic Circle and in the Interior. She is also an AMI Montessori educator. When not in the classroom, she is painting or writing. Her artwork has been published in literary journals from the West Coast to the East. She is also an internationally published poet. The great-great granddaughter of Joshua Slocum, the first person to solo circumnavigate the globe and author of the international classic, *Sailing Alone Around the World*, Susan carries both her pen and paintbrush across the Alaska-Coastal Arctic tundra and throughout its boreal forest. Additionally, she is the current Prose Editor for the quarterly journal, *Alaska Women Speak*. Lastly, but very significant, while she is (mostly) a solo adventurer, she joyously shares a home with a beloved other. It's all about balance.

About the Author

Kersten Christianson is a raven-watching, moon-gazing, English-teaching Alaskan, and author of four poetry collections: *Words from the Boreal* (Metaphysical Fox Press, 2025), *Curating the House of Nostalgia* (Sheila-Na-Gig Editions (2020), *What Caught Raven's Eye* (Petroglyph Press, 2018), and *Something Yet to Be Named* (Kelsay Books, 2017). She serves as Poetry Editor for the longtime quarterly journal, *Alaska Women Speak*.

Her poetry has appeared in various publications and anthologies. (Whitehorse, Yukon), Storyknife Writers Retreat (Homer), and Alderworks Alaska Writers & Artists Retreat (Dyea). She is also a 2024 recipient of the Lin Halterman Grant, awarded through the Alaska Writers Guild. This grant will go towards the purchase of a Little Free Library to gather and share the work of poets, especially that of northern poets. Since 2013, she has been an active member of the regional writer's group, Blue Canoe Writers.

Kersten lives in Sitka where she keeps an eye on the tides, shops Old Harbor Books, and hoards smooth ink pens.

Sheila-Na-Gig Editions

www.ingramcontent.com/pod-product-compliance
Lightning Source LLC
Chambersburg PA
CBHW020325130626
46549CB00003B/1020